Some Dredged Deep

Robin Wyatt Dunn

Acknowledgments

"what no battle ready," "gut the harp and string" and "dig and draw the deep for me" first appeared in *A New Ulster* #77, February 28, 2019.

"He's cutting the stems off the garlic" first appeared in *Doorknobs & Bodypaint #94*, May 31, 2019.

"I guess I never told you about Texas" first appeared in *The Metaworker*, June 17, 2019.

JOHN OTT
SAN DIEGO, CALIFORNIA
2020

ISBN - 978-1-940830-32-2

LOC - 2019904883

Cover art by Esmam La Crowned

By Robin Wyatt Dunn

POETRY
Poems from the War
Science Fiction: a poem!
Sunsborne
Wine Country
What Black Delirious Daylight Sets You Forward in the Boat
Remarriages
Debudaderrah
Black Heart Uprising

NOVELS
Los Angeles, or American Pharaohs
My Name is Dee
Fighting Down into the Kingdom of Dreams
Line to Night Island
A Map of Kex's Face
Julia, Skydaughter
Conquistador of the Night Lands
White Man Book
Colonel Stierlitz
Black Dove
City, Psychonaut
2DEE
This Isn't One of the Stories I Remember
The Black King of Kalfour
Sitting on the Floor

SHORT STORIES
Dark is a Color of the Day

PLAYS
Last Freedom

FILMS
A Wilderness in Your Heart
Party Games
American Messenger

for Olga

1.

I write to attack
tear down
rip open
and burn

I write to infect
destroy
and bake to ash

I right to unseat your apartment and your vase

I write to kill your husband

twenty miles out of town
steady drunk
singing a song in French

I write to insert antennae in your walls
singing in his voice

over your lids
my voice will paint stark alleyways
noir hips

the red blood of the damned shall pour over the Eiffel Tower
a stark and homely god.

I write to disinter the dead
and assemble their skeletons into notes
on my xylophone

2.

some whole night
uncluttered by evening
unremarkable except for the sky
open wide and bright

some whole night inside the dark of me
delight

bad-luck names and raging poems
terrible bright night inside

3.

what doorstop of a man
glads the hand of the tide
marked flaming over the divide

stubborn as an American writer

cutting into the sidewalk his name

madman in fine frame
to deliver the gift
from the river woman

some nicely colored rock
some story I heard

let me tell it to you

4.

burn the stake
and all the remnants of the poem
shake the ashes into the earth
spike the trees with your lips
throw off the cloak of history
and take your shirt into the cloister of the rapids' steam:

heave ho, on the dot
row the might out of the apartment
out of the description
into the broken red light flowering beneath the trees
blood and geese shaking their feathers in the stream

5.

ignite the cliff on my arm
burn me well
I have need of it
over my skin

open the freezing window
identify the pedestrian
twenty yards out
take back your arm with the rock

we shall stone the Canadians
in their homes

with cannabis and freezing whiskey
and rocks

and french rolls

shoving their queen up their arse
until they can shit only money

burn the ladders which reach my chest
fire your arrows to my battlements
I am Jerusalem
every dusk is mine

6.

what no battle ready; not in this life; it could have been anyone;
any scoundrel fit for the shaft; any body made to the order

of killing

and who are you now
watching it all
and laughing
my story-boy
kept-angel quadrarific
exceptional student of love

now name me the soapbox on which you will stand
stand there or die

give us this knowledge we crave
of your betrayal

7.

gut the harp and string out the innards for the park
each bandstand tuned in
for the song

too far apart
I can't see
come close to me

the waves of cloud are like the waves of blood under my skin
waiting for the electric charge

summoning my dark

gut the show and carry it on your back
eleven miles to sunup

each trap and knife and hat
for the surprise

I've got it for you love
the low light in your hands

down light

8.

this terrible bright day
shaking its landscape hair
over the writing paper
over the cerulean writing paper tempered over our hamlets
stark and naked
vomiting light

9.

dig and draw the deep for me
scry the shades of your beneath
whose arches and whose roads

tell me where Rome is
inside your mind

all the green sheaves of your silver shocks
rubbing over the surface of the walls
light

build me the machine to take me into the sky
and then the sky above that one
I want to see them all with you inside my mind

the river scrums the belly of the world
jet black and full
racing a current of cold love
squashing the air
charging your laughter with relief

before Rome was Rome it was a river
dividing one life from another
touching wet
each mark inside the dark a landscape all its own

I'm petrified to see the light spread out over the curves beneath the sea

10.

what a wonderful thing is betrayal
its innumerable shades fluttering about the ear
waiting for home

we feel it home in the chest
like some fatal keep
clasped under the waves
we sink

looking for meaning

the wonder of betrayal is laced over the eyes
and head
a science fiction circlet who shuts off the mind in iron.

betrayal happens more within than without
a feeling rather than an act
a consideration of the self
and who he meant to become
before he was this

betrayal's light hovers soft over the edges of the eyes' screen
waiting to leave its mark

11.

no raft or heft to help me
not any reason
not the shadow of a hernia
not the pressure of a doubt
strapped full to bursting
on the lane
kept trammeled and stacked to keep the fame away
all underwater

these poems serve to remind us of how everything passes away
the thought of yourself
the ritual of dying
the name of your dress
does your dress have a name?
does your cheek touch your sleep?

do dreams make sense?
and do we dream them?

which way is it
down or up
upriver or down
mainstay or bywater
have your ax
have your children
tell them stories

ruin the earth
there is always another earth
waiting to be ruined
every year
every memory
ruined

this beautiful ruin
shining out of the sun

12.

what terrible mountain
awesome and weeping
shakes his wings over the shadow of the earth,
sleeping standing
watching the night

the rivers run into him
in silence

13.

now night
and sleep
breaks the hold off my kingdom
moving me into the water

there are so many waters around
a thousand colors

black and white and red and orange
starling light

who knows the deep
who names its edges
who fills the mountain
who writes the name of the love of children
married over the mountain's edges
levering the seasons over their hearts
in scythes and sheathes

the dark of dream takes hold of your neck
and hold of your ass
and lowers you in to the sea

14.

sensurious
the shrike and stand of the winter colors
hum slow over the western horizon
striking the grave languid rush
of the north
curving over my window
& my home
to touch the future

15.

some deep desire hovers over the night
twenty years gone
it wasn't new york
it's some dead new york

shining simple madman hunted over the world
his face pressed against yours on the train
liquid ice

tell me the name of the station
give me the address
your love is bursting out of the ground
its milky frame
sucking in Charleton Heston
his white chest
cut open

tell me the meaning of the presence of our silent shakes
arming the minutes
bearing the color over the days

negritude's shock dynamic
silver's stretched Abrahamic lock
over the sight
onto the tight regard
of your frame
illicit and untoward

behold the night
his edges dream me into being

16.

now I am maintenant
maintaining my main net
over the revolution ocean

queue me the music
I can hear it over the wire
siss boom bah
striking the name

striking the harmony
bleeding
throwing me into the ring

who is it hurt you
ladies
and gentlemen

who was it said my name

close the main net
reel it in

reel in the Net

the silver fish are striking the surface of my retina

17.

now what have you been doing belly weight?
stuck in your ornery mass?
rising and falling
we know the story here
we know how you've done it
bright as a newborn babe
for us to carry on our back

18.

we'll knock on the ceiling
its red scope shaking the birds
humming deliberate over the sound
over the rational sound
of the beach

who makes the ocean grieve
and who divides the sky from day
who wracks the thumb
for its rewards
in making?

which cavern and which symphony rewards
the honest pluck
the daring scrape
against the bird cage
against the idea of us inside of it
numbing the throat
blasting the rational past
out of your ears?

I've eaten my toast
the sun scorches the light over the plain
the train is howling

what kind of music is it
when I touch my hand on the fresco
painted over the eye?

19.

no near and not every time
not near or rowed wracked not ready or Treme
not the black sundered strike sanding the next year
not the black time
and not the redoubt under the bridge over the water

this life
this lead life

shine my heels for this dance
give me your seeds
this winking hour

this pleasant beginning of war

bury my hands in the border

20.

dead night and darker heart
the spirit who divines the right
should keep me closer
but it's only me

the burial rite
putting the body into the ground
into the oven
up into the sky
into the stomach
into the ornament around the neck

the delivery of the flesh into the flesh

I write the rite now not right but getting closer

21.

don’t fear me
though it would make sense
like fearing death

I won’t know which hand to take

tell me when it’s over
the shakes over your face
like the sun

22.

never Friday
never Freia
not this Earth

shake the trees with my spite
iron out the kinks for our rage

I'm finding out the hard way
which way is down

23.

dead the row and dead the weight
and dire disaster in the taking under dear
we have it ready

no better end
and no better pain
can commingle in communion here with you
my bloody friend

I have my sword and I have the spirits who foretell this mastery
of art
still shrinking from the face of winter nights
like yours
overgrown with beard
the tomb and tear of my reward

give me everything you can
so I may sink beneath the ground
to find the wights and wedges of that other realm in dreams

24.

some secret source of terror light and reefed over sun days
straught over long night and lead; beneath the city small and neat
the sharks of my imagination swim the shadowy deep; no one
may keep the memory alight over the reef beneath the city steep
for I am still swimming there under the houses and the keeps
of hearts; the brown and red the white above; who burned the
lover's kiss over the surface of the shops and cars and churches
leaning round? it must have been some black dream inside your
head beating slow and rich beneath your eyes.

25.

beget that it should fall
how you mean it
when there is nothing else to do
dared delicious

slipping sideways into the gloom
to wait for its arrival

not a lover
or even a friend
but this absence

holding you close like a parachute
over the white

26.

the thought of death arrives in the brain and spills out over the body in rivulets
calming my hands

it is itself a kind of life: the thought of an end.
everything I do will be mentioned, not in words
only in ash

my head is a battery
fueling the habits and duties of my apartment

even the music
even my sweater

27.

we are arrived again
books in hand

the light shines through the window
the women wear practical clothes,
with some small adornments.

above us the administrators whittle their pens
watching the sky for signs of relief

below us the gardeners mow the lawn.

inside, the terror of the world finds its release
crawling out into my face

28.

the bronx has this color over the surface near the station
copper turned to the color of the sea
sinking sea green
I never found the building
but I can still see it in my dreams

hovering over the day in an interior night
not too far away;
just far enough to invite the imagination in

to what worlds of what that station never was.

it was probably just a dead factory,
closed since the 70s,

but it looked like something else

the hovering weight
the mast of a ship just out of sight
the nuclear drive of a forgotten warship
from a dimension too far to believe.

its copper edge climbs over the cityscape
in plain sight
but almost invisible
slipped under the reason of the inhabitants

shining in the weight of its sincere devotion
sheltering the silence beneath

29.

I'll break your neck
I have it in me to
This is the poem for it
wrapped around your neck
just a big necktie
for your morning

I love you

30.

terror and light
gale me with wishes
so many wishes
flattening against my window glass

both parts of me.
in terror, I write.
In light, I perform my duties as a man.

Perhaps writing is not a duty;
nor any treason either.
Just this whistling into the night.

31.

I held you in my hands
my wanderer
bright and sad
dutiful and full of honor
some bird bright against the air.

you are so full of these imaginings
the work of these years.

what did it make you do?
my brother.

what have you done?

standing stark alone against the silence
watching the rain

will you listen to it?
it wants to come in, to teach you.

but you'll walk through it wet
and not become what I'd hoped.
your picture of me.
Mine of you.

Canada.

See these drops become your eyes.
See the moon become your mouth.
Monstrous against the night.

who is it crying through your mouth?
Saying these unbelievable things in your cries?

what a wonderful possession.
in these territories,
my wendigo,
run like the night over the sandy snow
and scream until you are dead.

32.

what a strange shape the night is
like my heart
I poke away at it
to see what it is made out of.

what are you made out of, nightheart?

nightheart doesn't know
it makes a sound like an awning in the wind
or a ladle dipping in to the well

it hums this fruit
knowing all along things I don't know
it seems to want something
some iodine?

what is it you need, heart?
what masted rowship
storms over your embrace?

I have never seen the like
grown over me like a mold
under the earth
under the trunk I can see the sky
through the roots

33.

holy war
on my balls
in my teeth
in my scalp

on my tongue
my feet
my index fingers

my back.

34.

now burnt midnight
shredded cunts and cares
my beady holidays

wrought and wilted Saturnine silk

give me the cannons for the hill
and give me some bone I can hold between my teeth

each hour

now broken autumn shirks my heart
he never cared anyway
and the blood signs the light over the trees

take me into the wood
I have some evil in me for their work

35.

tintinnabulate and rise in my heart you murderer
sin selectively to sear my shrimpy muscles
starve my brain
(which way now?)

every way you can count
stuck and stomping my hands
pressing me into the hardtack couch

years for the ocean
placid and uncrossable
rising over my head
in harps

stamp the xylophone and scream a dying girl
underneath my ear drums
steel drums and F 16s to announce my death

loam for your garden
saints in the sky

aluminum over the bright steel cupola
staining your glass eyes

my chest is the timpani

36.

bear better Robin this life
who never knew you
except over the sight
beneath the drum of the heart

I don't know what things are
I don't know what orb or ornament ahead, above
watches quiet.

reason ignites
should he know
should he believe
stark or surf or sand the beacons banging beneath my eyelids

what are the sounds they make
what is the range of its bleeding

what is the destination of its iron peaks

37.

no storm delay
no winter
no time

not today
not yesterday
not this week

not with enough detachment
not ready for the gravitation of your sighs

here in the netherland
not netherlands

but netherland
waiting for some spring whose shape claws at the edges of the screen

whose wires slip beneath the doors
whose summertime is sleep
to shatter all who lie beneath

stare and stake the strumming rounders on their careered corrals
around our making
and if you want to
just give me some small piece of it to see

38.

what chains and heads shall muck about in our dainty splendor
the times cutting by the waste
the murders of the year
stuck over the burning cusp of these patiences
in musk

the dowry of the sun
is only youth
she burned better on a way;
she is a child.

over the iron sky are other ones
humming low and keen in their en-tumblers
and out of the earth are the ancient keeps and scrolls
written in forgotten languages we find in dreams

Keats is speaking with them too;
in his wanderings.

what color is it that we held when we were born?

and of what elements were forged the sky before this one?

39.

dear dead heart near me
should you ever be endowed with dark
some richer strange invention of the day

each morning
and then the afternoon
and night

tell me where it is
which part and cast of it
the pitiful enlastment of it
who instills
or merely remembers

the last part

of submission

sending under the brave burial dark
the memories that I had

dear dead heart
when you're at hand
when the dandy road ahead seems just too grand
invite me

and I will black every night you see
with sand

terrible and bright
illustrious and shining dark over the sea
for you

40.

dear heart begin
I have the wretched need again
silent in the stark delight to listen to the sounds of fright and
gravity these prizes--
shining soft over the valley of my bright

I have it in me now
who you were

41.

how many rages
shire sure and shared
who cages all the rare
and ochre sense and shape
all my families in deep
all the carriages are creeping close to speak
and I am dead
or near enough

all the winters of the hallowed haze
can mystify my rage if I would take them
or they can penetrate the deep and speak

which canyon and which corral
which serpent who coiled the rest and rake
of my patrimony
this absurd fairy tale
which arrogant fool
who taught my people all these dreams
burning inside me

which sallow revenant within my skin
is keeping me inside
to shout over this screen

which fairy fire willowing my heretofore horror
makes me drip my hands into the beast
bloody and proper

tell me which is fire
and which is ash
and which would you have

which is it brother
is it the story
or the life
tell me which word you'll bite
and bit
I'll see you spit
into the earth
before I reach for my kin
of iron

42.

who are you
and why
with your terrible closed eyes

give me the reason for your sigh
and shuffled feet
your crying and standoff

(ishness)

tell me who it was who taught you to crawl
were they so mighty and so wide
did you want to die for them?

43.

how now heart
how's about them hows abouts
bout that burn

stuck on the turn to doubt
leashed and watching for the curve of the sun's filament
turning about

blinking too fast to see

see yourself see your wile
cooling over the hot sea of your body

44.

sashay salute
without repute or honor
and in so doing
carol both
my caroler
Carolingian hussy and crew

bed and bake the name and rut
for these the burial rite of your past custom
over the sword of the Internet
over the passage of tribal will

scrape and sand the surface patches of your feet
here withal compete with me perforce for the armament of the word

45.

sail Robin you venture capitalist
you'll capitalize all the words
and be known in all the capitals
and your head
this head

will wait beneath the earth
for some geologic change
the logic of the earth
like the logic of language
squid like in its effervescence
squirting underneath the enamel
its urgent frequency of love

46.

who hearkens back to rue
this eventide like love
shapes the color of the sky
never right when you desire it
but still shining over the porch
a dim and bent metal lamp
from some previous century
lighting the path into the blackberries

47.

starry night within the bright and brittle casement of my mind
don't die
all my life is wide
limber shuckles strewn over the meadow
auburn and red
dead and dying

starry night
shuddering against the shutters
inscribe the dark lantern
and dive

your blinking eyelids cover the grass

48.

die, and live again
over the burnt and stuffing armature of your corpse
backed and brushed and bent into battle shape

who knights the talk of my feet
the pressure in my kidneys
the tension in my tendons
storming the citadel of my heart,
each arm wick looking for the pressure of the day
biting onto the brick grate of the house
the shade of the alley

nullifying the hate of love
to take the temperature of the lick and afternoon
of the route out

blast me into the tree
with your best gunpowder
the birds expect it

49.

what terrible victory
strumming his evil guitar
cut from Etruscan stone
standing over the river of time

singing in French
naked
holding his cock like some misfired weapon

celebrates the coming of Enlightenment

50.

Now send in the clowns from Los Angeles to clean up the mess; we've got candy on our face; I've got a hard-on for Holocaust and my main squeeze is dead (or near enough) on the other side of the Atlantic, and all the wars I've fought are being reduced into a machine-readable documentary-style utopia encyclopedia the size of a pack of cigarettes and these AGENCIES, ALIENS and AGENCIES, stuck to the bottom of my shoe, leaking fluid, demanding answers, propose that this message, and this afternoon, on Crenshaw, with forty nickels in my pocket, is the divine message I have been waiting for, because I am a Saint in a televised special available to be streamed to single 30 year old women, and because the long arc of consciousness, in coming to drip into our concrete vestibule, before the feet of God, and Sting, on Venice Boulevard where it splits, in the Y shaped traffic island, knows how urgently the disaster requires its resolution, underneath the Hazmat Dancers, sopping up the blood.

51.

Burn my children
burn and bake the buildings borrow all the staves and summer boots
shake your antlers through your hair under the branches

announce our coming

this is us
moving west

52.

what is the cost of evil
and what coin is it payable in?

what is the shape it takes
over your face
over my heart

who marks the trail of its incisions
stuck against the dirt
and weeds

in its hunger,
who is fed?

stay and fear my heart
nearing the avenue
hard and cased in judges

53.

The Canadians step wide
grinning insanely like a carousel mannequin

Lurching over into your lane
To say hello

"Hello," the boy says with a face like a cut piece of rubber

"Hi," I say

54.

growl for me so I know the weather
tell me how many hours till the men return
tell me how many days until the temple burns

near the blood
but far away from the swords
the writer sits
watching the stars tick

behind my back
the sacrifice

before me
the murders march ahead
over the plains of grain

55.

there are so many amazing things
once Samuel Beckett gave Andre the Giant a ride to school in his lorry
once I cut open a tire, just to hear it hiss

once the Masons only built churches
once a gypsy danced with me in Paris

once the sun burned over a world that was not this one

once the color of the mind was read

we can light the cathedral on fire
just to watch it burn
and you can love me, if you want

56

fever the ridge of your spine
over your hand
vibrating against the divine
shifted and scarred for the wire and sheep
kept auburn fire to burn the tracks and sighs
over the arch and creep of your rage
like the white sun
stark and raving curve

herd the shuddering cove of your belly
beneath the sky
liar armed with the tenement timbre of your voice

57.

terror over the avenue
like rain or fire in the air
shocked full and fine
her hair blue erect and dancing
over the lane
over the continent

here I am
blacked under the baked tonne weight
crushed but still muttering
words about her:

America began as a woman
and so she is in death:
howling banshee-faced
into the black hole of the West

will we love her better when she's dead?

58.

shake me slow so I can see the rooms in your soul
how many you've made
let me stretch out over your canvas fire
to observe your stars

exact and terminal beneath the stucco

the wash of light from the street
like the wash of the centuries of Los Angeles
—yellow against the black—
illuminates your nose

59.

tender fear and elicit love
illicit dreams out in the air
sucking in these freedoms
like the tide

shake the laundry out over the blood

60.

take all heed away
all of your thought
all your dreams just cast them away
you don't believe a single one of them

what good are your eyes in your head
or your ears
or your hands
what is that tongue for, if you will not taste with it?

you shut yourself inside
with these drugs
out of books
written by evil men and women
to torture you into death.

you stay inside there
as long as you like.

Some of us will miss you.

61.

touch the edge, hero
I see you hover over the film of light
somewhere your voice echoes back to me
and your finger

the radio sound--a mantra out of the storm--
splits the narrative into a dozen pieces
but all of them are centered on you:

laying your hand on the surface of the dome
and reaching through it

how many return?
Not all do, but some.
How to make sense of the shape of the world?
Like the shape of your hand.
Curved, and weighty.
Delicate.

I feel your pull out on the edge
Like a drip from my sea.
Tell us how far it extends.

62.

tell me the doorway and the key
give me the password and the push into the void

ten seconds in

and twenty

all of the darkness is like amber mercury
hovering over the surface of my skin

forty-five.

"what is it you want here, Robin?"

Answers, I want answers.

"what is it you want to know?"

I want to get America back.

"You can't get it back. You can only go forward. Build something else."

But who is going to help me?

"People already are."

Why do you have to have all the answers?

"I rage at night. My heart beats, like yours, though it is larger. Tell your friends I said hello."

Goodbye.

Up, up, up into the stars.

Back to my chair, with some little piece of me still stuck, over the abyss.

63.
Prometheus trembles underneath the heavy air
The shaking orbits of the sun and moon
The standard bearers in sky and on soil
Marching over his sight.

In the expansion of the mind,
Like the extension of the hand,
The universe shaves its dimples
Circling round the eddy of flesh
electric:

Star sounds and symbols archaic.

who is it to doubt the future--
to draw a picture never before seen?

64.

now sun me in your vale, woman
stuck on the hamper of your singing digs
stuck in the muck stirring the rafts of the months and years
shaking the beat hackling air in rising pauses
stark divides
your legs trace the winter coils around the stakes of the wood
each empire sound

grant me to leave this white sheet mind of mine
to help you
red and white dragons bent over your waist

65.

like death is a sword
love me
I can’t hear the radio
come again
please, come again

what is it you’re saying?
the sound of your voice is like the wind over the brakes
soughing pops and slow sounds
washed against my face

66.

the priest is kept inside, waiting.
outside, the snow is falling.
The church steeple is invisible.
The river frozen.

The refrigerator is humming,
like the music on his laptop.
A small piece of yellow paper covers the camera,
so that he cannot be seen, except by his ghosts.

He is kept warm by the blanket over his knees,
and the dreams he has at night,
of escape.

If god is inside him,
its language is Keats in Hyperion,
one syllable per year,
stretched out over the earthquakes and star storms and fights
with families, colleagues,
friends.

All the colors of his life.

what do his devotions mean?
these scribblings into the white.

& what is he waiting for?

67.

some roaming power left us
over the east
I feel it in my bones
over the ear bones.

I have it in me
the ancestor
whose names shine out over these trees.

what did we lose?
we left the den but gained the fire.

68.

what northern spring
regis and the light
scorned skullcaught like reign
hours knocking over the skipperwinter
glower lower:

all went norn-blessed
the white faces and dark hands
rhyming their terrible alms into the shores of the day

69.

there is a brown government building in Fredericton
like a sturdy shit
stuck into the ground
with bars over the windows
and chimneys hovering overhead

they have the same kind in Copenhagen
perhaps some Norse invention
scrawled overseas

underneath you can hear the children screaming

70.

the king hovers over your watch
laughing
he orders his men to search for your killer
while he holds on to your heart in his fist

71.

storm me for fire
however long you wait
in metered religion
aching straight
patient bear the syllabes to trace my lips over your chord

72.

whisperings numberless tumbled over the surface of the railing
inviting disaster, fame, ambition, love, pain, and other things
too thrilling to name

each adage of the door scuffled soft against the cheek in sleep
translates its poems into wordless susurrus
sleek, noble and deadly
ratcheting the night air

you, the transmitter
you, the crystal

summoned bright over the long deep must stand to see which
keep
which terrible light you'll see

73.

I carry a knife now when I come in to work.
I carry it close to my jacket.
It's good to put out someone's eye with it,
If they've seen what you've seen.

we can jerk the eyeballs around on strings,
play hunky dory
hari kari
yo yo rituals.

I've seen you bury your dead:
I like the way you are with a shovel.

Let me bleed for you;
I've been saving up.

74.

no black or white
no town or country
no vista
and no reunion

not this time
not the reason you came
nor the one you left

Not this love
or the one after
not enough
and not applicable
to the problem you have

not fully visible
nor really explained
not your problem
not this day
not the time you remember
not our love
nor this symphony
not the right or the yard or fate

something like justice
beating in your head
blackening your name
dragging you into the alley
shoving you full of drugs
lifting you onto the chair

to announce
god
renunciation
alphabets and poems
the lesions and weights of court
the end of the world
the end of humanity
the reason we came
the reason we're going
the punishments and the crimes
the restitutions for our deliverances
never enough

some white sun
some black dog
some sepia fever
stuck in a photograph

bark, damn you!
bark, rover!

75.

shock full of light
the country drive and white release
colored in the shade
bright and fading
cut into the dream like mercury over a NASA special
flying over imaginary planets
brown bows of grass
stretched behind the windshield
a holocaust painting.

the black between the lines invites in the hand
and mind

stuck over the sound of the being inside

76.

sign and shred me right
delight or dim reward, tight as a spell in the desert dark
on that lonely American highway infinite:

tell me how far to go,
and what kind of thing might wait there,
stranger far than anything I've ever seen.

who would balk to grin into the tangled skein of banks of worlds
strung out beyond sight
over the range of seas behind seas?

It can't be me;
if only I could find the friends to go with me.

77.

The American visits Canada

It wasn't that I told you to go fuck yourself.
I mean, I did say that, and I do want you to,
But that wasn't what it was about.

It's so funny, to see you after all these years.
How many has it been now? Two hundred.
It's almost like we're old friends.
Perhaps we are.

No, it was something else;
Not just I was reminded why we were at war;
why we had been shooting you.
That was clear enough almost at once.

Nor did I find you stupid-- no matter what I said.
I'm as stupid as you.
we're both stupid. I think you'd agree there.

It was that you were afraid.
You're still afraid.

I hate that you're afraid, so much.

78.

don’t leave me here
don’t chew through the wall
suck it off and spill it
right out the door

I have you here
on a trace
your face
inexact but graceful, mercury
the sun-born hue of the race
(whichever one)

burned over the pavement:

79.

the future shock is setting in
and already gone
the train left the station
zipping through my body like a ghost.

The bed weight gnaws my stomach
and it creeps over my skin
Looking for a way to get in:

To dream ghost dreams.

80.

what kind of a weak thing is Canada
what kind of a weak thing am I?

Canada is large
& I'm small
yet Canada is weak for being small
smaller than me.

my weakness is size:
too diffuse to hold on
(including to your hand).

America is about my size
a hard gun
a firm ride

but shrinking
falling apart
taking on water.

I must go to sea.

81.

redda redda runnabayguh
reddy reddy runny ready
red
riddle me this, my mother of fucks

why didn't you say something earlier?
You're too polite.
Too polite by far.

what kind of a truncheon do you think this is?
what kind of a mask?

what kind of a freeway gliding past?
Tell me how much
And for what
and I'll curse you just the right amount
to trust your judgment

82.

who heard the night
inside your fist
what dream did you have
stuck on the freeway
your hand lodged in the tarmac
looking for the reasons you came

tell me what it was
who took away your eyes

83.

Better underneath
The boundary's release
Like stormy seas under my pillow
Shake the hour I am dreaming of
vibrating yellows, whites and blacks

The bench of the town
The supermarket caving in beneath the onslaught of snow
(yes, there's still time to dance)
Radiating music from the horizon
Not so far that you can't hear
If you listen:

84.

telepathy is a kind of molasses
stuck to my cheek

85.

who heard the night when it was dry
locked inside your dying light
drifting over the sky to sheer the tops off of the trees
and your mind

all the remnants of our course should be carved out of the black
wood of the dark between the stars

86.

never again
never so bright
not the whiff nor warning of the night
carols stuck on spades and dancing
mourning the bitter year
and our orphanages
our orphanages increasing
numbered in the millions
trillions of lights
dancing wide under your feet

tell me you'll be home when I arrive
if only in sleep

the black mask of the future
wakes my pearl
summons the awesome riptide of the yearning whirl
broad and steed
named

87.

dead and gone
over the eaves
the reeve is silenced in the breeze tonight
along with all our corn
no melodies for us tonight
—we're torn—
between derision and delight
nowhere else to go:

I have it in me to describe you
though I've never seen you
why should I try?
what kind of thing did you earn?
these horrible wages.

watching quiet for the still in the heart.

88.

don’t torment me
I just want to know the address
for the door out of here

89.

Tell me the night
how far it is
how near and bright
the night insists it's killed me twice
never before so early or so soft

Get me run and ready stuck out making crinkling faces at you
Bloody and nice

90.

the particular color of blue-grey behind the green
swordmetal sky
shudders bright behind the night
watching slow for the raiment of fire in your year

91.

so shark tonight
dead hands and weary Apollo or Sauron
some lightkeeper
bark

stark bomb dread mere exact rip out over the sky

92.

ug bug brbrbbug bug
hey bugaboo
I've got everything you needed
Sharp as a tack
Mapped onto your face
Calculating
Calculating
Tell me:

How many more hours do you want?
And what are you willing to do to get them?

93.

fighting the powers that be
no enemy but within:
the grip of despair
anxious disease;

cracked and caught in our light.
pay me to deliver you
bright cherub
ornery woman
sticky man
shucking the nation's fables:

over the border, brother,
over every one
I can see that gleam in your eye,
who suffers the king,
who suffers the king within
marching in every war.

94.

name me the music of the heart
so bright and dark
which winter and surmise keeps you inside
summered and stark
lark on the watch and grave;

name the black ends and the broken kingdoms
name the ash:

silent and dreaming
bent over the breeze beneath
hell or some symphony
arcing round your electric head
arched fire and braking waves
splicing your hair

95.

don’t draw me out
I hold the rain inside
anonymous
dredged under the hull
molluscs and sea kelp
stuck to my skin

pining for the light to get in:
and it does:
slow

96.

take part
and wreck the lame and centered parapet of your thoughts
no never underneath
no bright or stalwart eye
inside

it's dying
to glimpse the light:

carols and chants part ways around your arms
dipping close to the whale-road of the morning air

97.

glow by me
I'm afraid
stark and naked in your rage
tell me how far to go
& I'll wait there

98.

what immeasurable cruelty
starves the fate of nations
carves the right out of the envelope of hate
noxious at the stop
turbine smoke

what kind of evil is it
who starts the car inside the heart
and drives through the fence

99.

tend wide
and sound the light over my eyes
right and turn the night over my sleeve,
love
no one else broad and steering evil beneath the freeway air
could catch bright and weary on the mainframe joy:

lark spinning time sings me the line from dreams
I've been trying to remember

100.

terror me the envelope
hours and streets going by
the tide of Canada
stuck on its mule's errand
bright and wide as a grave.

trade me the day
numberless and revenant
cut cold under the shadowed blue
trembling, like me,
before the waste of history

there is no more beautiful waste than history
only one moment behind

101.

striated canyons of the mind
chowdered heads of the strips of stars
brimming over the dark waste of the black barrier reef above

tell me, will you,
what keep you hold,
I want to touch it once,
under the agony of the cold,
to see your face against the darknesss

102.

bow down before death
he cuts your sleeve close
Lucifer and Night clutching your hand
illuminating the bright gulf of the world
swirling around your hands and feet

bow before the ways of death
numberless and serene
arching over every memory you have
over every dream:

the pitter patter of the rain beneath his feet
keeps you inside.

overhead New York is dead,
stuck cold in the winter,
unable to sleep,
and Los Angeles has lost its mind,
screaming itself into the deserts of its bed.

come closer to the numbers on his head;
the ripples on his skin;
we're done in beneath his cough and shin,
watching the world spin.

name me the night you knew as a boy
as a girl
when all was bright and wide
it's there inside
the name of the dark divide over your sleep

103.

tell me how close it was
was it close enough to taste?
or just a kind of memory half asleep?

I know it was some kind of sickness,
paid giving birth quiet in the night
a little blood and a little sigh.

tell me what to do
about the stand I have
two acres or so inside
ranging from my hands to my face

104.

a woman is a kind of thing we kept the din in
dark bark and bread.

the bailiwick beneath her bed
the burial chamber of her quickening hand.

tell me how you came and when
the numbers of your dead
tell me where you'll sleep and how's your head
how're your arms and your face
how the numbers read you here and led you to lead us bright and blind over the ledge

I knew every time you said it was dead that I was yours
clawed into the wool of your nest
for the feeding

105.

carry me dear
how close to think
the nip and tuck of the divine wind
starving my flesh to sleep

all the parrots on the hill are in
chanting my name

what is it again?

Robin Wyatt Dunn

like a seizure on the boat
stretched between oxfordshire and coventry
watching the light

106.

blacken and rage the engines in my hand, weirdo
knocking the breeze with my teeth
hardshipping sun braked to carry all the marvels in my face:

near the valley of your desk the books collide above your head
steering into your mouth
one by one we'll fit them in
inch by inch
to count the oceans in your fleshy face
for the photograph.

outside in the air all the students listen in for the professor's welp
red faces nourishing delight

weirdo, summoning the day around your neck
we'll arm the peasants with some songs
and a little dirt for their nails
the negative face of the silver sky
shudders to our hands

107.

stark white wheat
struck cold on the frame of the heart
close my eyes for the departure:

to the blood

108.

Canada died a long time ago
And I am the undertaker still dealing with this corpse
Arms and legs splayed over the cement
The head is ruined,
A pulpy anvil.
Eyesocket lakes.
The crows have been helping me eat it
But it's slow going as it's half frozen
Pitched into the Earth.

The penis still teases,
Threatening to rise.

The vagina a dark maw,
Hoarding spiders.

It still farts,
Politely,
Moving an ass cheek aside to let it rip.

This absurd task has been given to me by god,
And I am an insane cleric,
Marching around the interrment,
Barking orders at the yarmulked birds.

109.

The Canadians drive thick tired bicycles through the sludge,
gossiping about the women.

I have assembled a shotgun out of spare parts,
To hunt ghosts.

When the Canadians see me they leer, showing their teeth.

I make the sign of my people,
One hand over the crotch,
The other pointing at god.

110.

This one is for Amos Grieg

Death to America
let its righteous rain cut me deep
shovel its pain into the oven
to bake and make the peat
all one

Death to its bones and innards and cops
Stuck on the jock and rocking low
for water
onions
pearls
the whirl of the day

Death to its night
fast flight into the air
Not there but close:
The pallor and waste, the wracked balls.

Cackle with me in the fire
For our starvation shout:

Righting the lamplight out
To storm the fence

111.

Dead and Nailed!
Drunk and Righteous!
Killed and Maimed!
Bloody and Ridiculous

Drink for me in the street

112.

we'll burn you from your house
and wave the pages over your face
of all your beliefs
raging light

But what kind of punishment is possible after?
Do we put your body in the ground?
what are you willing to learn?

The mud has a kind of song to it;
perhaps you will listen to it.

113.

we'll set fire to your maps
that tell you where you're at
and take your cat into the trees to teach it how to fish
your burning wish I tattooed onto my hand
so I can watch it change

114.

You're obligated to go fuck yourself,
And I'm here to remind you of your obligation.

we'll put the crown on your head
and sing a song
right in your ear

louder and louder and louder
until you bleed

115.

Arm the mouth and lift the gate of the arm;
Raise the antenna over the head;
Lift the foot into the accelerator
Lean into the podium;
Charge the air;
Turn on the lights;
Cue the music, motherfucker

I SAID CUE THE MUSIC

WHAT ARE YOU DOING BACK THERE

YOU FUCKING BOURGEOIS PRICKS

Put a new round in the chamber of your heart
Patch the hull;
Raise periscope;
We are at 400 meters and closing:

The ocean closes around us
It magnifies
and changes:

the colors of the night:

Hold the note inside your mind
four meters streaming red
blood lozenges ripping through the milky air

I am your witness
deliver me into the prosecution
enter your statement
tighten your boots
hold your breath

I SAID HOLD YOUR BREATH MOTHERFUCKER

We're coming into the trees
into the Marianas Trench
there's a wolf out there and the wolf is you

So howl!

I said howl!

116.

The age of the winter
the mount of joy
the periodicity of despair
blinking in and out
cresting the hill:
waving from the treetop
his whip of blood--

the symphony of decay
mounted with bright daggers
putting the mountain through his paces
and rumbling:

stumbling around on the porch
making obscene faces
drunk on the sky
whimpering with mole-like sounds
face and whiskers in the mud

he raises his sword over America
grinning his toothless grin
somewhere in the Carter Administration
a broken train is launched into space
and into your window
400 decibels
vibrating your skull
with the names of god

117.

deliberate with me over the destiny of Mankind
these hands who work for money
bitter in the rain,
triumphant;

leak pitter patter over the wing of humanity;
while unrolling over the floor of the sky
and knocking beneath . . .

open the door to the tomb:

the water is leaking
into your shoe
the ghost is knocking against your jaw
ahead,
the screen drinks yellow images
coming from your mouth

deliberate and spell the deed dividing:
stick your mother's name to the stone hull shutting in your hand:

send the word to the water

118.

Poetry is a form of worship
for an evil god
that they don't teach you about in school.

He's not from this world;
He's a bitter tramp,
and friends with the devil.

He doesn't understand a thing;
nor wants to.
His jig is a sound I never want to hear
Even when it is coming out of my feet.

All the nations bow to it,
As they bow to children,
Grieving with mirth,
To show their faces.

In the child's eyes,
All the colors of the world are stars,
where the god is sleeping,
Unable to speak, or know a thing.

Sometimes I try to wake him up,
To hear him scream.
Then I will know I am an important man,
Taken into winds and harlots and mysteries.
But I am too stupid for him even to laugh.
His misery is some kind of color of the sky,
Pressed against my face.

It may be I will kill him,
And burn his temple to the ground.
All of the poets are hunting him,
Like monks for the Buddha,
Hoping for a clear shot with our rifles.

When we get tired we fight over the sandwiches.
Mark Zuckerberg is there, with his long face,
And we take turns dunking it into the lake,
To listen to him scream.
Finally we feed him too.
He does not understand,
And has not seen the god either,
who we are hunting.

I try to teach Mark to sing,
And he makes a sound like a broken piano.

Finally, the god arrives,
and pulls out some of the Jew's teeth to wear as a necklace.
It makes a horrible sound,
Like bodies in the surf.

I want him to look at me,
And he does, with his dark eyes.

119.

The spirit of the place moves over the sea
like a viscous nectar
nougat breaking:

the electrical course of the wiring line:
marching in to the sound of wine:

The English curl over their soup
growling incoherently
raising their arms
to warn the gods
that they are coming

the Americans are their gods
kept inside their pocket
smeared into light
leaking onto the street

the radiation increases
the names of the boughs
the identities of the spirits

the men are doing jumping jacks
and the women fornicate in the street
watching the tick of the dove
and the tongue of the frog

slipping under the diorama of the earth
the Devil is laughing

120.

The mutie father
And the broken son
Stare out over the landscape to take photographs

121.

The sound of your voice fills me with the rush of the river
Like an evil wizard in a movie, with electric hands.

122.

The fog is alive
sleeping over my forest.
he's coming back,
over the night,
watching for my shout.

inside of the dark inside his sleep
I'm waiting for the rope
to pull me out of the well

123.

dummy hips and broken change
deranged feeders for the culling
stuck sordid in the masterpiece
bright and dancing:

corded wrought and limited
too stupid to live
too needy to dry just yet:

necking on the category error
civilization
marking territory with the gap:
an urgent call

(the sound of my mouth a kind of black paint)

wreck the mainstay
and burn the town
I have it in me to record it all

124.

burn, my angels
and destroy
burn everything you find and see
heretics must burn
and we will hunt them
with all of our might
bitter and alone
dying in glory
over a novel
or a poem

burn the sheets
and burn the envelope
burn the reasons
and the morning
burn the flute
and the axe
burn the ending
make it last

125.

dream and die with me
never better
never behind the fire
out in front

never dream again
until you're inside the fateful train
plummeting below the reaches of the world
out of reach of men

stumble with me, dear
they're only nightmares
they're like us
wide awake

126.

drain the dark with me
the burial beneath the world
drunk and singing
shirking fire
for the cries of light
winking out from the horizon

the cloud of the night
is singing
so close to your cheek
a lover bloodied in the metal rain

127.

someday soon you'll get what you want
like a love truck stuck in first gear
watching all the world parade by

128.

are draw
drop might and ray
starve and shape the take
locked and brokered for the divine
relationship
starship

Narcan-ambrosial transit trip
underneath the setting sun:

carve and mash the ruin
barf and read the glowing yellow words above the library
block and hold the basement rhetoric
electrifying the air

dip down and reap the mighty steerage
of your worms
your words

129.

tentative hand
quivering beneath the air
held over the ravine

what kind of torture is the distance
and the recompensation
for the black array of love
marched into the heart to pray
and tear apart the walls?

what kind of village is it
whose language
spotted in the peaks
rivering the valleys
rushes over your tongue?

130.

bear the weight
and bury the men
bury the sand
bury the love you bear me
bury the will and the water and sand
bury the hand who bakes the bread
bury the man who takes his credit for the owning of it
bury the stall and shaking band
thundering the metal railings of the air:

bury the time
bury the meaning
and bury the fortune of your culling
it culled you and took you into it
ravaging your mask of a face with its words
riding over the highways
launching your rictus face into the television

bury the ship

underneath
all the songs will sing
out of all of your dead mouths

131.

the dagger dear diagonal
across your face
I keep it over my cock
a licentious arrow
for the meat:

what a treat it is
to see you smile when I draw it
so that I can draw you with it

132.

the lovers twist about the corridor
a wrist of years
turning over the fleeting glimpse of the reward:
neither future nor the past
and not the spinning world,
but the judgment of the spinning itself;
hacked onto the mainframe of the ebony lance
launched into air:

133.

big broadcast
hold me
we're falling into light
the sound has arrived in the air
held tight over the drum of the sky

irradiating the sound of my name
the sound of my body
the sound of my sons

every point on the compass
marking the pace of my movements
head to shoulder
fingertip to thumb

bring me the man responsible
I want to strap him inside it
and listen to him scream

134.

If sadness is electrical
Then churn me overboard
electrify my water so I can swim farther down

135.

hubba hubba
burning mama
cut out to stink in your drawers
the leash of life is short
and I'm gonna run you through
with my wart

it's a disease
this happiness
like the waters of the sun
come down to drown

136.

for Weasel

some days I dream of Texas
that never was
the one I was taught of
some Romance in the bathroom cut short
the dog and doggerel in the park
laughing at nothing--

some sweet song
when Texas still meant “friend”
that time inside the hallucination of the nation
who makes the feet tap
and the throat tighten up
for the words

137.

somewhere the sound of the 70s is playing a tin transistor radio
in a Canadian apartment that never figured out how to lose
or win
where the dream covers up your skin in linen
to drown you into sleep

138.

skin my sammy for the afterweight razor tar
stuck useless and at war
the mind of the enemy inside my own
demanding more:

give me the raisins and your wrist
give me the lift for the arch
stuck stupid and rafted wicked:

limpid disc shunted to the growling melancholy hip
armored to lisp the password into the sea:

stake my hand on the main band
I'll lift you up
each enemy I have is growing faster
hemp for my scythe

give me some gangster name
I can whisper in my sleep
Big Tony
Master Pink
Stinky Rafter
Onus Mountain
The River of the Deep Kept Under Your Thumb

I want more
Let me watch as you're asleep
I can feel you dreaming

139.

Burn the truth and watch it fade beneath your wing
I kept a piece that I'm never going to show you again.

140.

Dead me dreaming on the sea of you and me, not broken, not even really here: the estuary . . . all the peasants have an opinion, and I have one of them, and the music is playing: all of my music is playing and I plan to get more, wherever I can. Every calm sea is arriving, like matches to their fate, guests to the funeral, and I have no words at all for them, but there is beer. All of the pain has aspects of them in it; reasons and memories which I can't deal with now; perhaps I summoned them with it. Perhaps this is the end. What a beautiful end: guitar in hand, and cymbals, and the water, god's flood come to celebrate the beat. The ghosts are coming closer. Perhaps the ghosts are the music, or vice versa, and perhaps I am the winter, come finally to contentment, like a woman into marriage in some peasant vista, her name burned into the wall, and her oven made of the densest rock.

"Hey! whatcha doin there!" some kind of hick is in it; floating over the water. I too am a hick, not even armed except with years, and the apocalypse is merely our creature, a sort of vampire who follows orders, like we follow the tide, up and down the rivermouth; eddying and eddying.

"Eddy, come get a beer, I have something I want to tell you."

Eddy doesn't have to be told twice.

"What's that there you see?"

It's the light at the horizon. He's looking at it and so am I.

"That's the future, man."

It's yellow and blue. It's hot, and his skin is sweating. I close my eyes for the music.

141.

He's cutting the stems off the garlic, working and now there is no way I will not love him, even though garlic is merely a kind of vampiric propaganda as it thins the blood and so those who ingest it regularly are guaranteed to be easy to slaughter and bleed out; the piazza has no hours, nor any need of any, for even though the Etruscans gave it their clocks and times and gods the urgency of any Italic miasma feeds underground to the waykeeping mass of some five or six pre-Christian millennia— in other words, it's a kind of slow that has almost no heartbeat despite the deftness of his hands over the cloves:

Of course it's a factory hand, but from the centuries of factors, when a union was not something you carried a card for in your wallet, but a gang separate from allegiance to your city, and the dock an aspect of some Phoenician kingdom, pre-coinage, pre-imperial light:

thrust over every vista we can see. Because yellow is the color of madness because it is the color of the sun, but one whose face winds down under the hands beneath the skin into the gut, like his fingernails beneath the skin of the seeds.

I speak no Italian and the way of the piazza is closed to me; whatever ardor I have is swamped beneath my swampy ancestors, who would have regarded this clime with some form of ancestral terror, in its marching insistence on the right fluid make and marker of the lucent: but not now, not while I am watching him.

142.

no, dear
it all went away
the fear of the dawn
slipped underneath the sea

sometimes I think of you
and imagine what you'd do
if, when or but
out over the color

143.

Stupid Fucking Drama Queen

in the mirror

144.

I'm burning; never far; it could have been some dream I had when I was thirteen, and I was a hero on the ice sheet with a special name. The name was Face of Blayer; is it a silly name? Jason Voorhees for the Ice Age? Gilgamesh after the Fall; Beowulf, the whitest wolf that ever was, slipped into my sleep. The silver display in the near distance, like a fancy pool in Southern California, or an art gallery at the magic hour, light spilling out over the plaza; the fire needs to know my name (although it already does) and I should speak it, tell it why it is and where it was and how it'll be; which man it is who gave me my name, after my father:

it wasn't my father who gave me this name, nor is it the kind you can say with your mouth--it's somewhere in the spine, the residual pin of an anchor too deep to find . . .

the legions of light; this legion of light spread out in my mind, who comes ever closer to me like a nightmare; some coarse fragment of a disease, inoculating me to the expression of its mind, so I can only feel the edges of it, leaking over my skin:

what sort of thing is love, neither for man or woman, or even for a dog--it isn't agape, not pure or godly, nor eros for the hot body dreamed naked, it's the love for the sea when you're at land; the wish and waist of the sea over the southern california concrete, come to shape my mind in the shape of the afternoon light:

145.

not again
the pears are lighting up
the band has made a shape with its hands
like a heart
or a gate

and the sky is swallowing up the air

I'm walking again
like when I was a recruit

in the army of L.A.

the rhythm of the xylophone sounds like a parade
in hell

tell me who it is
I can hear you

what sort of thing is it you've been dreaming
each paintbrush

each shake of your wrist

the listing of your ancient ship
to starboard

the little dust on your bones
glinting in the night

146.

stuck
greedy and alone
bunched up on the telephone
to nurse the soil of stoicism
I've been laying away--

harking bracken to the leash I held in sway:
around my neck and in my hand,
to say
"all is grand, and I'm dying part of the band to say:

'bequeath and shriek. garrulous turn the microphone down to the ground and lead it the frowning substance overhead' "

147.

drainage ditch stuck up at the cuff
over the marmalade and seasonal presents
we present
on time
and in fashion
all the gruesome itineraries of the modern age
palpable lust
real honesty
& super clean things
stuck over your mouth:

things we can't speak of,
even when we want to.

when I tried,
the world ended,
and I ended up here,
talking to you.

losing traces of the soul
who brought us here:

mercury's love
nailed into my back
shining bright
over the forests of the black sky

148.

I guess I never told you about Texas, long and sweet in the evening, boiling jelly, about mom's temperature, stuck in the oven:

The best and worst part of the Texas was its nights, serenading the broad-backed racial fear of the destiny of men, and some of the women (though they were generally less worried about destiny), and the arch-send-out of the reigning spirits, incandescent over the lives we'd built in our hollow; never enough; never American enough; nor hardly even American, and bent into the wind to see this reason—what reason is it? —what kind of nature could it be to hold us so, spinning as a bright metal top in his hand, and hers: melted over the asphalt.

You never saw us wrenching out the sockets from the street games and startled faces of the hard-worked adults, shaking off their pores into the distance: the black-bottomed arrow-boat of the majesty of years, stuck into the grime and ant-colony waste, a lyrical prison, carefully swept of some of the dangerous sharp objects and casually maintaining some of its others, magical:

We shouldn't say too much. Shouldn't wait too long. Shouldn't mean too much when we say it. (Though I do). Pretend I mean nothing by it, and the return of my hand to yours, just to say hello, or goodbye, is a kind of anchor whose channel is so deep it can hardly be noticed; the earth.

149.

starve each reason
stare and burn the careful craving
shackled and nightmarishly serene
unstoppable
black and ebony ruins
blackening the base and burial site
numinous
monstrous
my heart

150.

all my molly
cancer causing gentle
the soda fountain of hate

carried five meters
tell me why
it's all inside
the will to die
and the life inside
trembling over your feet

this wheat is stumbling along
waiting for your poem
it won't be long
it's yours

151.

the longing itself
like the brakes
only hold out so long

152.

Seminar

the beginning
we slip into the chairs
I'm holding shut my eyes
the people are talking
the feelings start
inside my hands
the old man is speaking about death
I try to record what it is
that he is speaking about my death

the woman is watching the winter
color her face
and I am watching her

each of us is waiting
like devils in church
for a follower to come
and brush up against our cheek

153.

there once was a stupid woman
who thought that she would be loved forever
and that a poem written for her was worthless

those poems are destroyed
and they were bad

were they bad because I was a stupid, bad poet?
or were they bad because of her?

this is a stupid poem about her and me
and what you get when you don't get what you want,
which is most of the time

here she is, getting another poem
one to tell her
what kind of thing she is becoming

154.

death and destruction
mighty rivers
ancient peoples
and my heart

riches unconquerable
light
names
fountains of faces
ripped over the side

give me the gun
name the man who has to die
here is his death
like a small hole
in the side of the island

here is my heart
wrenched over the side

where are you, Atreu?
Rasky?
The landlady is back.

I have a telephone line to the Merchant of Death
His Highness
Coming in on The 12 O' Clock News
Richly Swerving around the cones we have placed on the Stage

His Name is

His Name is

Dammit, I forget what his name was.

He was the guy with the guillotine.
Luckless and afraid
More beautiful than the sky.

with silver skin
and a smile like lightning

let's call him Raskolnikov

brittle as an axe
white as my mother

reaching over the side for my cock
reaching into the heart of the mountain
for the mother

155.

Melt the sky
and hold my hand
for the rush

tear the noose
and hold the brush
for this excision

blood and manure
wreak my tomb
into your face

suck my thumb
for the thwack
and tack the names onto my back
for the eruption

I am a tree made out of fire
spurting into your homes

I am the name of your failure
written into your grave

I am the love you never met
coming into your home with a knife

to cut your children an egg
with salt

to carve your aegis
above your bed.

this is your epitaph

here lies my enemy
nameless
in a grave with no bones
that I wear as a hat

here is the null
giving your mother the righteous judge

156.

which one was it
who hurt me?

let's not count them.
it could have been either one,
or one of their friends.

the justice is still distant
perhaps it's just a kind of granola
that keeps for a while:
sweet nuts.

don't tell me how far it is
it's so close
like your face

157.

hold out your passport
stand in the rain
this is your seat
here is your name

here is life
watching the people move into the spaces arranged
fires

flickering beneath the eyes

hold on to the pole
wrap your scarp around your neck with the other commuters into
the dark.

hold on to your pocket
write down your name
write down your face
tell the man everything

here is my hand
here are my teeth
here is the shell shocked shape of the riot keep
here is the name of the infinite deep
creeping behind our bodies.

stand beneath the band in lights
flying over the arc sodium night

here is the name of my life
one moment stretched beneath the reddening sun
circling the white beneath our feet

158.

arm the name I had inside
for the thing that comes beneath
and arm the weights over my shoulders
and beneath my feet

stake the tent for the wait in weeks
outside the suspicion we've been nursing
that something is coming:

159.

all my life
in pornographic detail
hanging onto my balls
over the iced sidewalks of Canada:

you've heard about my balls,
and their outrageous size,
and I assure you,
as your mother assures you there are no bright demons lurking
beneath your bed,
that their truth divines a righteous energy
to find just where to lay me down:

over the street.

Canada, still a medieval village,
retains its savoir faire for matters of the heart,
leashing them to their foreheads,
like obscure philacteries,
that they stroke absent mindedly in public.

Yes, the Canadians are Jews,
thrust from Noah's Arc like unwanted mistresses,
onto the galactic ice sheet,
baby seals:

Club a Baby Seal to Make a Deal is what the television says,
in the salacious accent of Charleston or Tallahassee,
ruinous and stark as a winter wind.

what is the relationship between my balls and Canada?

is it your heart?
bleeding out?

let's just shake them for a while,
with the television off,
like Michelle with her lover,

finally free on the sands of the beach we never knew could exist
when the cameras were on.

160.

stand and salute the capitalist within
the terrible emperor, with his brittle teeth,
hands steady on the rail.

watch and create the space for the decay of your enemies,
the names of their destruction pregnant beneath your skin,
inviting in the regions secreted and dim, in love:

shake out your hat and scarf,
and settle in,
for the long night,
bright beneath the fluorescent lights and cameras,
to find the friends who'd died.

drag them out from the soil,
and breathe into their mouths.
to let all the demons out.

wraith keeper priest of mine,
tick the minutes out till their eyes are shining.

161.

no one else
but you

this time
not this time
but every time
with you

not every time
but this time

162.

Dare my shredded mind to see
the names and shapes of all the things on me
sunken in the midnight sea to swallow dark and light together:

the ordinary day
wrapped under the rain
wondering how this came to be

163.

Now boundless with rage
If we should part,
Me with my sanity and you with your habit,
bristling and popping under your waistcoat,

we should fuel the night,
anarchic
and holy
rubbed over our faces,
loam and blood

the grand arbiter
shining dark over the sky
his dimpled hat
frightening in its simplicity

we can draw every curve
of your dress
of your enemy's dress
and watch for them to meet
in the alley

164.

All the names of my fathers are dead;
Like twinkling gems,
Thrown into the sky.

Their sound is the air;
blasted into a shape.

Their letters are spelled
like seasons of stone:

raging deep trunks diving beneath the soil.

165.

now I have been made
alone and by fire
twisted into shape
a weapon
for the masses to use.

which mass is it pushing me to the wall?
the white wall of heaven,
crumbling beneath my hands.
like chalk.

My grandmother's name is chalk
the white wall of Dover,
but there were others before her.

what does the tool understand about what it does?
we know our enemies: the hands who hold us into the fire.
and the hands who hold them,
quiet and warm in the sky.

166.

no stormy light
no winter cheer
not the melody
not the judgment come icing like the flame
not your speech
buried cold in the night over the silence of the courtyard
and not better music
shining over your skin

the electric gun
medicating my mushroom stem
burying the sky beneath the spinning imagined shapes
you threw to me
over the years

the electric gun
welded to my brain
demanding the buildings wrought from shame
each one of iron
blasted round and pushing my needs
towering around my head

it sways beneath the sun
its carol pounded bright
limning the edges of my neck

167.

Here we go

wire down the feet
turn off the targeting systems
bend the knees
damp the lights
watch for the red sheen beneath your hand inside the rage:

each instant in time

each body armed with the fire of death
each man

arced triumphant

paint the wall with your joy
bleeding white

168.

lief means beloved
as your hair means grace
the after ace affair stark naked and erased
from the grand state
not anywhere I'd want to be:

who mans the standing in and to
in the red light

and & who gives out a kiss
after all the lights are gone

169.

it's coming closer in
the fear
like weather or laundry.

who feels it shiver underneath your chin
just an invitation to look in
(to the dark)

I'll sink into the bottom of the boat
and watch the black sky
twinkle white

170.

now die, like legions of saints devouring their arms and hands and feet, sink in to sleep:

sink in to serve the stark and wintered keep of mine
(I've been keeping it for you)
black and raging
each part in order

I need your counsel:

all around the falling fate the eyes and fish who swim above us sing about the trust
the stapled and ignorant trust we broke
the burial rafts are being readied
and the black sands are awash in my mouth
look at the grains:

each one glowing
I sweep them under the door but they keep coming back into my mouth:

you see the arrow and the slate
draw for me how to understand the fire

171.

who's singing to Los Angeles?
It must be me.
My dead city.
Like Lucifer wasted in the night.
Junkie in the alley
screaming:

My beautiful burnt heart.

wait for me for the ear
the bark chides my sleep
charcoal cheek

the lights burn dimmer in the deep
swimming over my head

if I haunt you,
if I should scrape the door;

of your eternal nightmare;

your sigils wrought with fire

your names a head and a wreath

your bodies the rocks of rats

your writings
the testaments of ants

awake and sing of your death

172.

what fearful light
the light of rage
a coruncopia of light
falls over my skin

stuck on the walls
rising over the melody to light the rays and change the timing of the dawn
each instant stuck and shoved in to the grate
lighting up:

brilliant denouement
red white hair

173.

I hear you calling
this work of my imagination
bright strokes of the drum:

which narrow band of my mind
will serve to quell the nuisance of it
the bald and bearded kingdom of love
nighted over the force of the land
some silly hat
the dunce and wizard
father

174.

make the maker make you soup
charge the hummer in the brakes
name the father of the hand
staple the apple over your band
endure the cruelty of the youth
and bark the shadow
ecstatic

the prayer beneath the tree
and the ghosts of the tribes who fled
(inside)
watch you

sight the battery of your thoughts
check your timetables
this is the gun

you are my enemy
hear my punishment

we're taking the names out of your children
and giving them new ones

175.

no black night
not my punishment
not the soul
not the river
not my life

eat the hand
and cure the sick
watch the rick burn

light the fable for the boy
and shine a halo for the girl

deck the halls with gasoline

falalalalalalalalalalalalalala

all the embers stark and red
embed my hearing in your lead
like leashes on the fog of your regret
holding back your will

not the resolution
and not your part

not the need
and not the juice

the listless wrist
shined and forwarded
midnight pale
starks me to the sunless vale of you

176.

husband water porter priest
hatchet carry lumber sheet
wash and ready slumber marry
eater stand and favor
carver stapleton and frame
baker pitcher pickle itcher
scurvy melanoma shame
shame eater
my shame eater
come in
pumpkin parker painter pixie stain
no long refrain from you, eh?
is it so yet?

Canada

ox and hue and rake
parchment scraper stipple take
and lay it out on the rue
orchard basement
glad mask
basket barfer

come in

177.

heaven is the arc of sky
and hell the deep below
iron both:

John Lennon means “gracious lover”
The first name Hebrew and the second Irish.

The iron stretches around his hand.

178.

for Kate MacDonald

the silver lit sky's a stark reminder
ash trees shove into the base to redeem the patter
and patience struck under the crown:

all leashed to the world.
we scry into the deep only to name the things we
already see
black chalk and white paper